SONG FOR HIS DISAPPEARED LOVE

CANTO A SU AMOR DESAPARECIDO

BY **RAÚL ZURITA**

TRANSLATED BY **DANIEL BORZUTZKY**

ACTION BOOKS

NOTRE DAME, INDIANA 2010

ACTION BOOKS

Editors JOYELLE McSWEENEY & JOHANNES GÖRANSSON

Art Directors ELI QUEEN & JESPER GÖRANSSON

Web Editors JOHN DERMOT WOODS & EMILY HUNT

Editorial Assistant KIMBERLY KOGA

Graphic Designer ROBERT McKENNA

Action Books gratefully acknowledges the generous support of the College of Arts and Letters at the University of Notre Dame.

Action Books

356 O'Shaughnessy Hall

Notre Dame, IN 46556

www.actionbooks.org

Song for his Disappeared Love /Canto a su amor desaparecido

©2010 Daniel Borzutzky, ©1985, 2010 Raúl Zurita

Excerpts from this translation were published in *Action, Yes* and *Mandorla.*

Canto a su amor desaparecido was originally published by Editorial Universitaria (Santiago, Chile, 1985).

The Spanish version in this new edition contains revisions.

ISBN: 978-0-9799755-7-8

Library of Congress Control Number: 20100924235

First Edition

Song for his Disappeared Love was originally published in 1985, a brutal year in Chile. The government of General Augusto Pinochet, the dictator who came to power in the 1973 military overthrow of the democratically elected President Salvador Allende, still ruled with terror and violence, kidnapping, torturing, killing and disappearing those who spoke out in protest. For Raúl Zurita, then, the situation called for the unreachable goal of "responding to the terror with a poetry that was just as powerful as the pain being delivered by the state."[1]

Zurita knew from firsthand experience what this terror was like. He and several hundred of his classmates and professors at the leftist Universidad Santa Maria in Valparaiso, Chile (where he was completing a degree in engineering) were arrested on September 11, the very morning of the 1973 coup, and he spent the next six weeks deprived of communication with his family, incarcerated on a military ship where 800 prisoners occupied a space that could only hold 100. I had once read that when Zurita was arrested the military officers were especially suspicious of a file of poems he had with him, and when I had the chance to meet him in April 2009 he confirmed the story for me. Specifically, the military officers didn't know what to make of the illustrations accompanying the poems. They thought they were secret codes and in response they beat him. Eventually, a senior officer recognized that these were 'garbage,' mere poems, and as he casually tossed the writings overboard, he took from Zurita "the only thing that told me that I wasn't crazy, that I wasn't living in a nightmare... and when they threw the poems into the sea, then I understood exactly what was happening."

The pages tossed into the sea were from Zurita's first manuscript, *Purgatorio*, which he had committed to memory, and which he did not return to until three years after his arrest when he finally felt capable of writing again.[2] He eventually published the manuscript in 1979, and since then he has steadily put out several poetry collections that deal directly, both personally and communally, with the horrors of the Chilean dictatorship. Along the way he has picked up numerous accolades, including the National Literary Prize of Chile, and he can safely be considered one of the preeminent voices in Chilean, Latin American and Spanish-language poetry.

In addition to his written work, from 1979-1983 Zurita was a member of CADA (Colectivo de Acciones de Arte), a political art action group whose projects included *Ay Sudamerica* (1981) in which airplanes dropped over Santiago hundreds of thousands of flyers proclaiming that "every man who works to better his living spaces, even if they are only mental spaces, is an artist."[3] The next year, 1982, Zurita returned to the sky to craft what is perhaps his best known work, a poem entitled "La Vida Nueva," written with an airplane above New York City, and reproduced in photos printed in his book *Anteparaiso*.

When I asked Raúl about how he had come up with the idea for sky-writing poems, he told me that originally he had tried to get the Chilean Air Force to execute the project because "if these same guys who bombed La Moneda (the government palace where the democratically elected president Salvador Allende took his life during the 1973 coup d'etat) were capable of writing a poem in the sky then it would prove that art would be capable of changing the world." Surprisingly, the proposal was not dismissed out of hand by the Air Force; it worked its way up the bureaucratic ladder to a commanding officer, who eventually shut it down.

---

[1] This and some of the other passages in this introduction are from an interview I conducted with Raúl Zurita on April 3, 2009.

[2] A new English-version of Purgatorio, translated by Anna Deeny, was published by the University of California Press in 2009.

[3] This is my translation of the text from the "Ay Sudamerica" flyer, which can be seen on the website artechilenoindependiente.cl as part of an article entitled "Ay Sudamerica" (1981)/otra repuesta más a "Los artistas bajaron del columpio."

It is worth mentioning here the symbolic importance of airplanes during the Pinochet years. On one level, there is the 1973 bombing of La Moneda during the coup, and on another there is the nightmarish reality that throughout the dictatorship bodies were dropped from airplanes "into the sea, lakes, and rivers, or dropped onto the Andes."[4] In other words, the bodies dropped from airplanes entered the landscape and became a part of the country's 'natural environment,' and this is reflected in various places in *Song for his Disappeared Love*, particularly in the refrain: "All my love is here and it has stayed: / Stuck to the rocks, to the sea and the mountains/ Stuck, stuck, to the rocks the sea and the mountains." These words, incidentally, are inscribed into the Memorial for the Disappeared in Santiago.

In his over 30 years of publications, the natural world reappears persistently as an entry way into the cultural and political realities of Chile, and when I asked Zurita to comment on this, he said: "For me this is a mystery. It's a mystery, I don't know. The truth is I'm a city person... but I began to feel at one point that in the face of the violence and horror that nature had something permanent. That it existed before and it will exist afterwards... but why? But why so obsessively? I don't know."

For Zurita, then, nature shapes and defines its inhabitants just as everyone who lives under a dictatorial governmental is shaped and defined by its terror.

"To all of us," writes Zurita in his dedication to *Song for his Disappeared Love*, "we are tortured, pigeons of love, Chilean countries and murderers."

In many ways, the placement of the tortured alongside of the murderers is the perfect evocation for modern-day Chile, where former Pinochet supporters live and work alongside former Pinochet opponents, a situation extraordinarily exemplified in the story of how Michelle Bachelet, the Chilean President from 2006–2010, herself a torture victim under Pinochet, found herself thirty years later in an elevator in her apartment building with a neighbor she recognized, Marcelo Moren Brito, the secret police colonel who had abused her in the aftermath of the coup.[5]

It—the torture, the disappearances, the fear, the violence, the loves lost—tortures everyone. Everyone lives with it no matter what their political affiliation. The shame and guilt, Zurita might say, is communal, and it cannot be escaped given that the blood and the remains of the disappeared are scattered throughout the landscape. Of course, the reality of violent societies marked by killing, torturing and disappearing is common throughout the Americas, and this sense of international shame is reflected in the "niches" section of *Song for his Disappeared Love*, where the rigid, prison-like shape of the text frames and forms its content.

Finally, while it is easy to situate *Song for his Disappeared Love* as a political response to a particular moment, it is important to keep in

---

[4] The quoted passage is from President Ricardo Lagos' 2001 speech which for the first time officially acknowledged that the Chilean military dropped bodies from airplanes, which was known for many years but never formally recognized by the government. Lagos' formal recognition of this fact forms the starting point for another of Zurita's books, INRI (2003) that was published in 2009 by Marick Press in a translation by William Rowe.

[5] For an explanation of the Bachelet/Brito anecdote see Tina Rosenberg's New York Times May 11, 2004 article "Chile's Military Must Now Report to One of its Past Victims." Also, Ariel Dorfman's play Death and the Maiden (1991) presents a hauntingly similar situation.

mind what the title makes clear: this is a love song: a song not just for lovers split apart by disappearance, but for love that has disappeared. In this sense, the book's anger, for me, at least, is as present as its generosity. And though this might stand outside the usual range of the translator's note, I think it's worth saying that in my experience with Zurita over the past few years I have been struck by the generous way in which he has approached the inevitably awkward and clumsy act of translation.

I first contacted Raúl in December 2007, when a publication had asked me to translate a few of his newer poems. I'd been reading his work for years, and so this invitation provoked both excitement and nervousness; and when I wrote to Raúl for the very first time to ask him to clarify a passage, to my great surprise he replied soon after with a new version of the poem he had revised after considering my question. To be clear: he knew me not at all and certainly my name or reputation would have meant nothing to him, and yet he trusted me enough to re-write the poem.

From a translator's perspective, then, this openness has allowed for a sense of creative risk that I hope adequately reflects the spirit of Zurita's work.

DANIEL BORZUTZKY
CHICAGO
2010

SONG FOR HIS
DISAPPEARED
LOVE

Now Zurita — he said — now that you got in
here into our nightmares, through pure verse
and guts: can you tell me where my son is?

To the brothers and sisters

To the mothers of the Plaza de Mayo

To the association of family members of the disappeared

To all of us, we are tortured, pigeons of love, Chilean countries and murderers

I sang, sang of love, with my face soaked I sang of love and the boys made me smile. I sang louder, with passion, and dreams, and tears. I sang the song of the old concrete sheds. It was filled with hundreds of niches, one over the other. There is a country in each one; they're like boys, they're dead. Black countries, African and South American countries: they all lie there. With love I sang pain to the countries. Thousands of crosses spread across the field. His beloved sings with her entire being. She sings love:

It was the torture, the blows, that broke us
into pieces. I was
able to hear you but the light was fading.
I looked for you amid the ruins,
I spoke to you. Your remains
looked at me and I embraced you.
Everything ends. Nothing remains.
But dead I love you and we love
each other even if no one understands this.

– Yes, yes, thousands of crosses filled the field.

– I arrived from far away, with tons of beer in me and

– the urge to piss.

– That's how I arrived at the concrete sheds

– From close up they were vaulted barracks with broken windows, and they stunk like

– piss, semen, blood and snot.

– I saw mangled people, men pecked with small pox and thousands of crosses in the

– refrigerator, oh yes, oh yes.

– I moved my legs and called all those putrid dudes

– Everything had been erased except those two damned sheds

– A wicked prince tried to grab me from the waist, but I called up his number put it on the

– grass and fled

– Then they blindfolded me. I saw the Virgin, I saw Jesus, I saw my mother

– skinning me with blows.

– I looked for you in the darkness but the little beauties could see nothing beneath the

– bandage on your eyes.

– I saw the Virgin I saw Satan and Mr. K.

– Everything was dry in front of the concrete niches.

– The lieutenant said "let's go," but I searched and cried for my boy.

–   Oh love.

– Damnit, said the Lieutenant, we're going to bleed a bit

– My girl died, my boy died, they all disappeared.

Deserts of love.

Oh love, broken we fell and in the fall I cried looking for you. Blow after blow, but the last ones were not needed. We dragged ourselves a bit between the fallen bodies to stay together one next to the other. It's not tough not the solitude, nothing has happened and my sleep rises and falls as usual. Like the days. Like the night. All my love is here and it has stayed:

– *Stuck to the rocks, to the sea and the mountains*

– *Stuck, stuck, to the rocks the sea and the mountains*

– I travelled to many places.

– My friends were sobbing in the old concrete sheds.

– The boys howled.

– Let's go, we're at the place they told us about — I screamed to my beautiful boy.

– My face dripped and the gentlemen joined me.

– But I found no one to say "good morning" to, just some witch– men with

– Mausers who ordered a good blood bath for me.

– You're crazy, I told them, don't believe it, they said.

– All that could be seen were the crosses and the old sheds covered in something.

– They clipped off my shoulder with a bayonet–blow and I felt my arm as I fell to the

– grass.

– Then they hit my friends with it.

– They went on and on, but when they beat my parents I ran to the

– toilet to vomit.

– Vast prairies formed in each bit of vomit, the clouds

– breaking the sky and the hills getting closer.

– What's your name and what do you do they asked me.

– Look you have a nice ass. What's your name nice ass little bastard bitch, they

– asked me.

– But my love was stuck to the rocks, the sea and the mountains.

– But my love I tell you, is caught on the rocks, in the sea and in the

– mountains.

– They don't know the damned concrete sheds.

– They are. I come with my sobbing friends.

– I come from many places.

– I come crying. I smoke and I get the boys really hot.

– It's good for seeing colors.

– But they are digging us up by the doors.

– But everything will be new, I tell you,

– oh yes beautiful boy

– Of course –said the guard, we have to yank out the cancer by its roots,

– oh yes, oh yes.

– My disembodied shoulder bled and the strange smell was the blood.

– Turning round you see the two enormous sheds.

– Traces of T.N.T, guards and thick barbed wire fences cover the broken windows.

– But they never found us because our love was stuck to

– the rocks the sea and the mountains.

– Stuck, stuck to the rocks, the sea and the mountains.

– Stuck, stuck to the rocks, the sea and the mountains.

– My girl died, my boy died, everyone disappeared.

Deserts of love.

They dumped limestone and rocks on us.
For a second I was afraid they had hurt you.
Oh love, when I heard the first bang I stuck to you even more.
Something happened. I am sure something happened.
I felt the stones squashing you and I thought you would scream,
but no. Love are the things that happen.
Our dying love does not go away.

I was collapsed at your side thinking that I was the one who threw myself over you. The grass will be growing, I imagined. In reality I prefer the stones, I thought, no, the grass.
I thought it was you and it was me.
That I still lived, but as I crawled over you something from your life denied me. It lasted a second, because afterwards you crumbled and the love grew in us like the murderers.

It's sweet and not.
It was the last crack and there was no need to move.
Now everything moves. Your pupils are still,
but four infinitely open eyes see more than two.
That's why we saw each other. That's why we speak to each other,
while with your spine you support mine. And even if no one sees
it, I thought this would be good, that it's fine. That it would be.

Now everyone is fallen except for us the fallen.
Now the entire universe is you and I minus you and I.
After the blows ended, we moved a bit and destroyed I was the only one you felt come closer.
Now no one will know, but it's you I look for, who I care for.
Weeping for you perhaps we are all one thing.
Now I know it but it doesn't matter.

– Oh, the great glaciers come closer, great glaciers over the roofs of our love.

– Hey *ronca*, screamed my beautiful boy, the dinosaurs are getting up. The helicopters

– descend and descend.

– Where the old sheds lay, the high walls with T.V. towers.

– You could appear on the screens, oh yes love.

– In my dreams I switch on the dial and you appear in black and white.

– I say: that's the boy who dreamed, that's the boy who dreamed.

– When I awake there are only casualties on a large patio and scalps

– hanging from the antennas.

– Listen friends — I shouted — those days are over. They just laughed at me.

– They marked the boys and with bayonet– slashes they cut their hair.

– Do you smoke marijuana? Do you sniff neoprene? What shit do you smoke you

– filthy red?

– But they're beautiful. Even then I'm able to see them, I wet the bed and smoke.

– I fall in love with them, I make myself pretty and put on my face. Drenched in

– tears I greet them.

– But today everyone dreams the dream of death, oh yes beautiful boy.

– Great glaciers come to carry off the remains of our love.

– Great glaciers come to swallow the niches of our love.

– The niches are one in front of the other.

– From afar they look like blocks.

– I saw it all as they beat me, but I swerved and my guard could not restrain me.

– There I saw colors and I saw the true God screaming from inside the

– frozen concrete sheds,

– howling in the ghostly concrete sheds,

– soaking myself completely in the impossible concrete sheds.

– Chilean mule–my mother insulted me — soon your time will also come.

– I swerved all over and without moving from there I saw my parents.

– They are like God.

– But they don't know their puppy is dying from love and blows in the old sheds.

– Now they look for me the cold stiffs.

– Impregnating us, young and old alike, with thick wads of spit,

– we burst.

–   Oh love we burst.

–   Oh love we burst.

– The South American generation sings folk songs, dances to rock, but everyone is

– dying blindfolded in the belly of the sheds.

– In each niche there is a country, they are there, the South American countries.

– Great glaciers come to pick them up.

– White glaciers, yeah brother, they creep closer above the roofs.

– My girl died, my boy died, they all disappeared.

Deserts of love.

I cried and I sang. The howling dogs chased the boys and the guards laid siege. I cried and harder as the bodies fell. Black and white I cried the song, the song to his disappeared love. I cried all my despair. The grass is as high as the niches. I said to the country boys take this, take my shame and it will switch off.

We sang our nostalgia for the countries, for the Chilean country. There was a trial and a sentence, we crossed the other niches and in front of our country's the psalm exploded. All the shame. The entire psalm fell on your missing love. The entire procession sang with nostalgia. For them, for the dead countries I said no, it didn't hurt.

The countries are dead. One shed is called South America and the other North. I saw torture, I said as I opened myself. We sang the prayer for the dead. My whole evil star then sang the song to my love who was leaving. Many crosses were called and went. All the paisanos I said crying she's gone. She's gone, and I don't suffer, no I don't suffer.

The Internationale of the dead countries grew larger, ascending, and I gave it my love. I gave it all my country love and I added all my cries and then the General of the dead countries called. That's how I bled the wound and as it gushed red the song to their disappeared love started. All the letters were opening up like graves, the scream the country said no it didn't hurt.

– Singing singing to his disappeared love.

– Singing singing to his disappeared love.

– Yes my beautiful girl, my beautiful boy, it's my karma, right?

– All my countries and hometowns call to my love, my beautiful fallen boy.

– They're all there, they float in the niches

– All my boys are destroyed, it's my karma, right?

– I am soaked all over and I love you completely.

– Singing, oh yes, singing for their disappeared love.

– Singing, oh yes yes, singing for their disappeared love.

Argentina, Uruguay and the Chilean countries of my true and disappeared love. Through a staircase one ascends from one country to the other. Through elevators one ascends or through airplanes of love that also descend into the shadows and sometimes also ascend. You and I walk there. We walk between the graves talking: Did you eat me? Why were you hungry Chilean did you eat me?

Didn't it sadden you? Flowers from the central country changed and I was dying. At your side I died and they put me on top the way the Argentine countries are on top of the Chilean. Each one ascends one atop the other: Niches from the dead American sheds call out. They kill us — I say — from the sadness and they call.

I loved you, I loved you so much, she says, all of the black night whistles and I held you with my hand and you saw it. It's something that only the dead would do. Yes you have to be dead to see each one of these letters opening into niches. Letters, little letters, she says, tombs of missing love he says. I held you with my hand and you saw it. Did you read the letters, the little letters: Missing countries, he says.

From the disappeared love the countries are also called. Buried in the walls they rest like us. They massacred the boys and the countries remained. We are them, she said. It was tough. Some are nicknamed the starving countries, from the central wastelands or the good USA in the American country. The others are behind. My love: we were eaten.

The end. And then:

.... Then an explosion oh my beautiful boy oh my beautiful girl I saw you further down and we are both dead it's my karma, right? Let's go beautiful little boy come now and see the love I sing to you it's all in tears and flowers yes come with me now. Cut. Come with me now my sea of stars. Cut. Oh yes my little guy come with me now. Cut. Come now, read and continue. Cut. And then:

The paragraphs read and say:

The headlights filled the road. Everyone cried out for mother and father's love and as the doors to the ascent opened the ballad began again. For his disappeared love he went from hole to hole, grave to grave, searching for the eyes that don't find. From gravestone to gravestone, from cry to cry, it went through niches, through shadows and it went like this:

The central countries cried. Their deaths were marked by date, time, and name. They were found in Barracks 12, in urns that indicated the cause of death. When they were raised in humane countries and animals obstructed the rivers but they were friends. They obstructed the jungle, but they were friends. They obstructed the nightmares and they were like days. This was before. They cried the whole night and they lay there. The bomb is black. Amen.

South American countries that cry. They have this every day, suffering and devouring countries in Barracks 13. In sandpits, Indian cities and worlds were massacred with no shame, friendship nor law. They died from love hunger in dreams that mark and name. They lie and rest in peace. At night they emit light and wail. The origins and complaints are noted. Amen.

Araucan niche. They were found in Barracks 13. They were long black valleys like the others who disappeared. It was noted: Southern airplanes ploughed the sky and as they bombed their cities they lit up for a second and dropped. So it says in barracks on engraved tombs that warn. In the limestone they erased the remains and all that was left was the final wound. Amen. They all broke into tears. Amen. It was tough to watch. Amen.

Amazonian Niche: in the darkness the game of shadows was sent to the space and corridor of the Barracks. There was a battle and cross with the Peruvian and Brazilian countries. It was said that the encounter left blood, and the great deserts of Sao Paulo and the Amazonian sky. It was said that it was a river of death and Paraguay. The blood pushed against the gravestone. It says: rest and stay. Amen. It does not state a date. No, it only states a Cross.

USA Niche. Found in Barracks 12. Northern countries and dispatched to eat themselves up thanks to their dreams of special shields, of murderers of blacks, of domination. They descended the sky and they called Hiroshima the country that blazed; Central countries, valleys and Chilean gluttons. The graves are nights and everything is night in the American grave. They rest in peace like the bison. It was a Navajo phrase. As it was written, Amen.

Argentinean Niche. Shed 13, a ship beneath the country of Peru and above the country of Chile. From torture to torture, disappearance to extermination, a hole was left and it was like the aforementioned countries and the night had nowhere to fall and neither did the day. Country disappeared from the horror behind the barracks. From there the wind blew across the inexistent pampas and as it settled the massacred faces became visible, Amen. Tombstone 6. White skin is all it says.

Peruvian Niche and mountainous regions. Like all those referred to the Barracks and Ship these countries lay the Shining Path and extreme misery. In planes they rumbled a road of light through the Urubamba and the ruined raised their candles. The groan emerged from cholai: Oh the evil of my Peru, it says, they're all tombs. They cried more than the others and now it's a dream and they lie. It groans: it's the "A" of vistas.

Columbian Niche and the white countries. Arranged in groups. Aisle, barracks and number stated. In the sierras they fell rattling and all the people were the first death. Then, when the city of M19 turned the sky red, the mountains accompanied the fallen and in this way Colombia became a snow storm of the dead and fallen. Rest in peace went the love song to the whites. Black is white. So it goes, it says, and it cries.

Central country Niche. Little by little the light was throwing shadows and as it arrived here it changed colors. The evening fell. The countries sunk in silence but beneath the niches one heard the sound of rivers and beneath the rivers the scream of the fleeing Indians. Then came the blood bath and the rivers sounded just like the rumbling bombers. The end. Santo Domingo died, rivers, lakes and green jungles. It reads: we were good.

Paraguayan Niche. Referred to Barracks 13. Another massacre between countries, Chaco wars, and La Plata wars, condominium and suffering. Now it lies in its niche surrounded by barbed wire, aisle and tomb. It says: I rest for the Guarani Marcos, and the whole song was sung, it says the niche. It says: I sing for peace in Paraguay, I sing for the shot down helicopters, for the Ipacarai country who kill with cane. All of this has ended. The niche says day and it bled.

Niche: dear skies of the Carribean. They died and were assigned to the hallway of Barracks 12 and 13. It was the last sparkle on the horizon, the last glow. Thousands and thousands of pieces dragged along begging, then they sang, finally they got up and saw the tombs open. Like the great moon the sky shone another instant and shut off. It was the void, the black rag of Carribean love. The epitaph says: it covered everything.

Niche: forests from the Alamo country. They blazed, crumbled, and were not assigned a particular niche. They remained in countries and rested. Enormous airplanes destroyed them touching their burning love. The forests burned from lasers, chemical warfare, and nightmares. They cry, it says, they were scalded. The flesh is ash: so it is written. The jungle is flesh: so it's written. The jungles are burnt bodies: so it is written.

Niche: the country of Haiti and sky. It says: dear central and American skies. It was not the same blue, it was lit by stars, and everyone prayed as they looked up at it. It was the great naves, the voodoo and missiles against the stars. On setting, something from the blue of the sky turned violet, the cold purple of the corpses. Now, the blue sky is the eyes that searches, the island that searches. No, they are black graves, they are gone. In the niche it says: I curse his sky.

Niche: volcanoes from the Guatemalan earth. This is what we call the Guatemalan tomb number 14 and it says: Dear corn field of my country, dear volcanoes of my country, dear blue of my country. There was no, it reads, need for extermination nothing fatal no murder. It was dead, corn and lava. The date stayed in Mayan and the glow of those corn fields was never known. No one knows. Like Peru it cried; dear corn field, dear craters. It rests.

Niche: desert of the Mexican country. It lies beneath New Mexico. The Mexican desert first covered the walls with sand, descended with thoughts and as it arrived at the plaza, rulfos and students raised their arms. It was packs of hounds and massacre, more managed to climb the steps. The climb is longing and prayer, it says, but that's how the image remains. Mexico '68 lies. The stony ground is the niche. It says: neither arms nor legs, beloved God.

Niche: Colorado desert country. Same as the last niche. Same as all the other stony grounds. In handwritten print the gravestone says: My God has dark faces. Long brown plains undulated, but it wasn't the wind, but rather the tanks and the love-thirst that moved. They begged, but only the maroon replied and together they fell into the canyons. The northern desert fell. Niche 16. Dear red sand, it now said.

Sandino Tomb and the green lakes. It says God, it says Nicaragua beloved night died. In the niche one sees: sieges by air and sea, electronic, contras and sabotage. They kill the boys at the border. Dear entire lake Nicaragua it climbed the volcanoes and fell like a deluge. The fallen covered fields. Now everyone is gone. Sandinos and countries. Nicaraguan niche, it's called, it's number 17. Beloved night, it reads.

Niche Venezuelan Tomb. Bolivar's niche, it says. Gravestones, tombstones of the third world — what we used to call the countries. Niches from the American Countries, new American or countries that smiled at the greenness. Goodbye, they say. They all form part of the designated shed. It was black, like the rails on the oil tankers in the sea. This is the Venezuelan niche. Only one human rests there. There's neither oil nor earth. Dammed night.

Alaskan Tomb. White is God. The countries of Barracks 13 were seen only as whiteness. Ice of the Eskimo country, the white elk and rivers. It was the 19th seen. The dead plains raised their grasses for the last time over the countries of Canada, USA, and the other frozen ones. Their love fell in the cold, their hunt was frozen and the tribe stayed in the white niche. It's there. Death must be sweet in the snow. Amen.

Tomb 20. Country of Cuba and islands, malecón and islands. Described one sees: Mountains and mountain ranges, are they there? Lakes and lacustrine, are they there? Thread and spinners, are they there? Indians and Siboneyes, are they there? Blockade and blocked, are they there? The Mariel Bridge, Havana and reefs, are they there? They read and stopped. From the whole scene the cry fell and the sound: the beloved island died. The sound: USA, Cuba, and Marti's country, dead in peace like the bison and the grass.

21. Bolivian Niche says: my love is the entire plateau. Signaled in Barracks 13 and aisle. In the disappeared love from La Paz there remains in the Aymara tongues a pain so deadly of the pigeon who died battling. It says this: from defeat to defeat the most beloved was digging out the grave. Bolivian nation, it reads, capital Lechín. At night, in dreams, the beat of the silent plains stopped. Chazki delivered the good-bye amen and stop.

Tomb 22: Country of Ecuador says: beloved are the mountainous, Amen. Niche and Police Station also assigned. It says: it surrendered to famine, a load of brothers and suffering. Of Shuar and Quechua in cry one reads: Central country and jungle of fiery birds fluttering and whistling the whole hymn of their disappeared love. Love by day, and love by night that in the gravestone now says: Dead birds and greenery. Jungles and snow storms.

Tomb 23. Country of El Salvador. It says: have mercy for your dearest Salvador. In the shed and epitaph it reads: Nothing was so much, nothing was so much, nothing was so much. House by house, the one who shed the most blood for the people lies beneath Honduras and above Guatemala. When not even one was left it exploded, singing the way he sings to his love the song of the disappeared. Everyone sleeps now. They dream and sleep. Like the stone. Amen.

Niche 24 of the starving Chilean and Argentinean plains, Chamarritas and pampas. There are four assigned to one. Return: they are pieces of the Argentinean country that did not fit into the niches from the barracks of the Navy, Quelmes and Villa Grimaldi, Baquedano and Dawson form the Chilean niche, Amen. The disappeared love in each tomb, niche, and name says: nothing.

Niche 25. Uruguay country: cries for the love that does not find, also signaled and noted in torture, shooting, and disappearance. Tomb that changes — it reads — with the color of the eyes of the searcher. So it reads in the Uruguayan niche, the burial of their missing love, of their disappeared and end stop. Rest your eyes that search and don't find on the Uruguayan sky thus the dead Charrúa, says no, we don't find, no.

Easter Island Tomb of the countries. Niche 26. The territory does not inform. Only the bird who crossed borders and countries lies there. Like the toucan, that's how Easter Island lies. We were raised there, they say, just like the flock, just like the valleys they face, the mountains they face, the long beaches they face. We were born here say the dreams they face. Islands of disappeared love, it says. Everything; islands and countries crying nest and niche.

Tomb snow-covered niche 27 of the countries. It grew from the love we had, the tomb reads. Frozen with the love they had they climbed the mountain ranges with snowy peaks and the white crests could be seen from the sea. In the sheds there are mountains and seas. The largest is as high as the South American and North American mountains. No, they are barracks surrounded by sea, they are islands surrounded by sea oh no. Don't leave.

28. Oh don't leave, he groans. Andean tomb of the countries. I'm going, away, everything dies. Everything dies sucking itself. There were as many mountains as there now are clouds. Grey clouds. Blacker and greyer rising in the sky, climbing and evaporating. Those are the mountains. Holes in all the countries expanded downwards and the torrent of their love was the rain. The mountains rained, says my Andean darling, don't go. Don't go, she says.

Don't go this is only death. 29 of the countries. The darkness began to rise over everything. The night squid that went around detaining everything and there was the sound of the song, the cry, the rain, of their love all the brothers are the Song, the Song for his disappeared love. I'm going, *run run*, little angel. The Chilean countries and all the others named. It still cries for the hole formed from the missing love from the missing homelands: Are you calling me?

30. Is the tomb of the country's love calling? Did you call out of pain? Out of pure pain? Was it out of pain that your love cried so hard? They told me so often that it's over, that it's all over and that it was the dream that was over. The brother says I saw you lost on fleeing grass, little countries, says the niche. Lost in the blackness everything disappears in the islands, names and countries, yes; are they calling me? Are you calling me?

Barracks 12. Aisles and niches, indicate the location of countries divided and marked oh yes it says, crying.

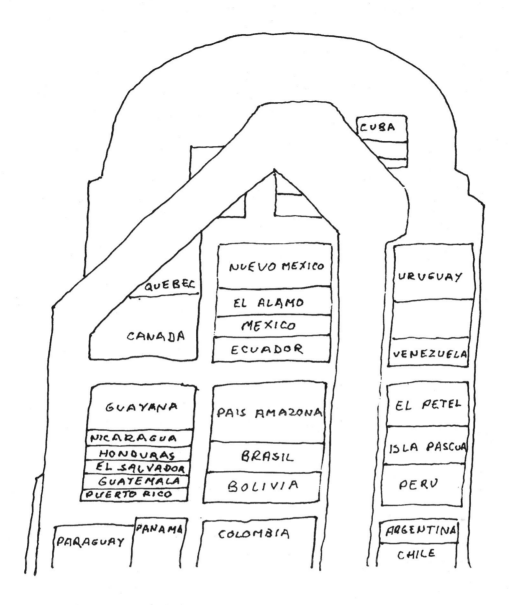

Barracks 13. Aisles and niches, indicate the location of countries divided and marked oh yes it says, crying.

Do you remember, Chilean, when you were first abandoned as a boy?

                                                            Yes, he says

Do you remember the second time when you were about twenty?

                                                            Yes, he says

Do you know Chilean and pigeon that we are dead?

                                                            Yes, he says

Do you remember your first poem?

                                                            Yes, he says

he says yes yes yes yesoooooooooooooooooooo

ooooooooooooooooeeeeeeeeeeeiii

iiiiiiiiiiiiiiiiiiooooooooooooaaaaaaaaaaaaa

la   la

            la

howl to singing

The night sings, sings, sings, sings

She sings, sings, sings beneath the earth

Appear now!

rise anew in the dead little countries

Chileans, karatekas, somozas and traitors

Rise up and deliver again your flight and your song

it's only because of you brother that it flies, sings, and takes shape

yes return it to this one the most tearful and the most poet

disappeared from love

pigeon and evil

Yes, he says

RAÚL ZURITA studied engineering in university. His early work is a ferocious response to the Chilean September 11, which took place in 1973 when Pinochet took power in the coup d'etat. Like many other Chileans, Zurita was arrested and tortured. In the 1970s he helped to form the radical artistic group CADA, and he became renowned for his provocative and intensely physical public performances. In the early 1980's, Zurita famously sky-wrote passages from his poem, *The New Life*, over Manhattan and later (still during the reign of Pinochet) he bulldozed the phrase *Ni Pena Ni Miedo* (Without Pain Or Fear) into the Atacama Desert. For fifteen years, Zurita worked on a trilogy which is considered one of the signal poetic achievements in Latin American poetry: *Purgatorio* was published in 1979, *Anteparaiso* in 1982, and *La Vida Nueva* in 1994. Other books include *Poemas Militantes* (2000), *Los Paises Muertos* (2006), *Poemas de amor* (2007), *In Memoriam* (2008), and *Cuadernos de guerra* (2009). Raúl Zurita is one of a handful of the most important contemporary Latin American poets, and he is the recipient of numerous awards, including the National Literature Prize of Chile and Guggenheim Fellowships. In 2009, Zurita's *INRI* (translated by William Rowe) was published by Marick Press, and *Purgatory* (translated by Anna Deeny) was published by the University of California Press. Zurita lives in Santiago, Chile and works as a professor of Literature at Universidad Diego Portales.

DANIEL BORZUTZKY is the author of *The Book of Interfering Bodies* (Nightboat Books, 2011), *The Ecstasy of Capitulation* (BlazeVox, 2007), and *Arbitrary Tales* (Triple Press, 2005). His other translations include *Port Trakl* by Jaime Luis Huenún (Action Books, 2008); and a special issue of the *Review of Contemporary Fiction* devoted to Chilean fiction writer Juan Emar. He lives in Chicago

Sí, dice.

¿Te acuerdas chileno del primer abandono cuando niño?

                                                        Sí, dice

¿Te acuerdas del segundo ya a los veinte y tantos?

                                                        Sí, dice

¿Sabes chileno y palomo que estamos muertos?

                                                        Sí, dice

¿Recuerdas entonces tu primer poema?

                                                        Sí, dice

dice sí, dice sí sí sí siiiiiiiiiiiiiiiiiiiiioooooooooooooooooooo
ooooooooooooooeeeeeeeeeeeiii
iiiiiiiiiiiiiiiiiiiiioooooooooooaaaaaaaaaaaaa
la   la
          la

La noche canta, canta, canta, canta
Ella canta, canta, canta bajo la tierra

¡Aparece entonces!
levántate nueva de entre los paísitos muertos
chilenos, karatecas, somozas y traidores
levántate y lárgale de nuevo su vuelo y su canto
al que sólo por ti paisa vuela, canta y toma forma
sí devuélveselo a éste el más poeta y llorado
desaparecido del amor
palomo y malo

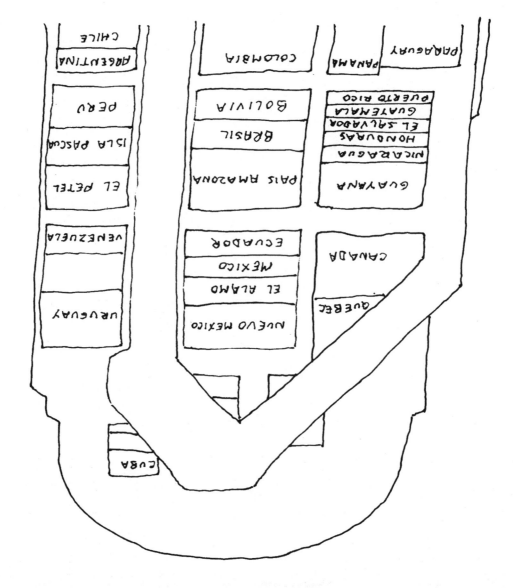

Cuartel 13. Pasadizos y nicho, se lee ubicación por países rayado y marca ay si se dice, lloramos.

Cuartel 12. Pasadizos y nicho, se lee ubicacón por países según rayado y marca se dice, lloramos.

Nicho 25. País Uruguay: llorado del amor que no encuentra, signados y referidos también en tortura, cacería y desaparecimiento. Tumba que va cambiando —se lee– por el color de los ojos que busca. Así se lee en nicho Uruguay cavado del amor ido, del amor desaparecido y término. Descanso al cielo uruguayo de los ojos que busca y no encuentra. Muerto entonces el charrúa, dice no, no encuentra.

Tumba Isla Pascua de los países. Nicho 26. Territorio no informa. Sólo el pájaro que recorrió fronteras y países yace. Como el tucán, así yace Pascua. De allí crecimos van diciendo, igual que la bandada, los valles del frente, las montañas del frente, las largas playas del frente. De allí nacieron van diciendo los sueños del frente. Islas del amor desaparecido dice. Todos; isla y países lloran nido y nicho.

Tumba nicho nevado 27 de los países. Creció del amor que tuvo, anota la tumba. Heladas del amor que tuve subieron las cadenas de picos nevados y fue entonces el penacho blanco que desde el mar se ve. En galpón están montañas y mares. El más grande es la altura de las montañas América del Sur y América del Norte. No, son cuarteles rodeados de mar, son las islas rodeadas de mar ay no. No te vas.

28. Ay no te vas, gime. Tumba los Andes de los países. Me voy, larga, muere todo. Todo muere chupándose. Hubo tantas montañas como ahora las nubes. Nubes grises. Más negras y grises por el cielo subiendo, escalando y desvaneciéndose. Esas son las montañas. Huecas de todos los países se largaron para abajo y fue el torrente de su amor la lluvia. Llovieron las montañas dice la andina vidita no te vas. No te vas, dice.

No te vas que es puro muero. 29 de los países. Entero fue subiendo así la oscuridad. Calamar de la noche que fue apresando todo y sonó el canto, el lloro, la lluvia, de su amor toda la paisa son el Canto entonces, el Canto a su amor desaparecido. Me voy, run run angelito. Los países chilenos y nombrados todos. Llora todavía por el hoyo que queda del amor ido. De las patrias idas ¿Me llamas tú?

30. ¿llamai tumba del amor de los países? ¿Por duelo me llamaste? ¿Por puro duelo fue? ¿Por duelo fue el amor que lloraron tanto? Que tanto me iban diciendo que se acaba, que se acaba todo y fue el sueño el que se acababa. Perdiendo dice paisa te vi por pastos que se iban, paísitos dice el nicho. Perdiendo negro todo se va desaparecido por islas, países y nombres sí; ¿me llamas? ¿Me llamas tú?

Tumba Alaska. Albo es Dios. Sólo de blancura se vieron los países en Cuartel 13. Hielo del país Esquimal, de los blancos alces y ríos. Fue el 19 de los vistos. Las llanuras muertas alzaron sus pastos por última vez sobre los países Canadá, USA y de las otras heladas. Su amor cayó en el frío, heló sus cacerías y las tribus quedaron en el nicho blanco. Está. Dulce ha de ser la muerte en la nieve. Amen.

Tumba 20: país Cuba e islas, malecón e islas. Descrito se mira: Sierra y serranos ¿estarán? Lago y lacustres ¿estarán? Hilo e hiladoras ¿estarán? Indios y siboneyes ¿estarán? Bloqueo y bloqueados ¿estarán? Puente El Marial, La Habana y rompientes ¿estarán? Leyeron y pararon. Desde toda la vista cayó el llanto y sonó: murió la isla amada. Sonó: USA, Cuba y país Martí, muertos en paz como el bisonte y el pasto.

21. Nicho Bolivia dice: amada es toda la meseta. Indicada en Cuartel 13 y pasillo. Del amor paceño desaparecido quedó en lenguas de aymaras un dolor tan herida la palomitai que cayó guerreando. Dice así: de derrota en derrota la más querida fue cavando esta fosa. País Bolivia se lee, capital Lechín. De noche, en sueños, paró el latido de todos estos llanos callados. Chazki larga el despido amen y chanta.

Tumba 22. País Ecuador dice: querida es la montañosa, Amen. Cuartel y nicho también consignado. Dice: sucumbío ante hambrunas, carga de hermanos y padecimiento. De shuar y quechua en llanto se lee: País central y selva de pájaros de fuego aleteó silbando todo el cántico a su amor desaparecido. Amor del día, de la noche que en la lápida ahora dice: Muertos pájaros y verdores. Selvas y nevados.

Tumba 23. País El Salvador. Dice: ten piedad por tu más cercano Salvador. En galpón y epitafio se lee: Nada fue tanto, nada fue tanto, nada fue tanto. Casa por casa, la que más tiró la sangre del paisa yace bajo Honduras y sobre Guatemala. Cuando ya no hubo uno más explotó cantándole como a su amor el canto del desaparecido. Todos ahora duermen. Duermen y sueñan. Como la piedra. Amen.

Nicho 24 de las hambrientas llanuras chilenas, argentinas, chamarritas y pampas. Son cuatro asignados en uno. Vuelta: son pedazos del país argentino que no cupieron en nicho referido en cuarteles de la Armada, Quelmes y Villa Grimaldi, Baquedano y Dawson del nicho chileno, Amen. Llorados de todas en una tumba cupieron, Amen. Del amor desaparecido por toda tumba, nicho y nombre dice: nada.

Nicho: país Haití y cielo. Dice: queridos cielos del central y americanos. No fue el mismo azul, porque estelado, todos rezaron mirándolo. Fueron las grandes naves, vudú y misiles contra estrellas. Ya al terminar, algo del azul del cielo fue el violeta, el frío morado de los cuerpos. Ahora el azulino son los ojos que buscan, la isla que buscan. No, son negras fosas, están idos. En nicho dice: blasfemo su cielo.

Nicho: desierto del país mexicano. Bajo México Nuevo yace. El desierto mexicano cubrió primero de arena los murales, bajo por pensamientos y al llegar a la plaza, rulfos y estudiantes alzaban sus brazos. Fue jauría y masacre, mas lograron subir unos escalones. Es ruego y ansia el subir se dice, pero así quedó la estampa. México 68 yace. Pedregal es el nicho. Dice: ni piernas ni brazos, Dios amado.

Tumba Sandino y los verdes lagos. Dice Dios, dice murió Nicaragua noche amada. En nicho se anota: sitiados por aire y mar, electrónica, contras y sabotaje. Matan a los muchachos en la frontera. Querido todo el lago Nicaragua trepó sobre los volcanes y cayó como el diluvio. Los caídos cubrían los campos. Todos ahora están idos. Sandinos y países. Nicho Nicaragua se llama, es la 17. Noche amada se lee.

Nicho: volcanes de la tierra guatemalteca. Así se llama la tumba Guatemala 14 y dice: Querido maizal de mi país, queridos volcanes de mi país, querida selva azul de mi país. No hubo, se lee, necesidad de extermino ni fatal ni asesinato. Fue muerte, maíz y lava. En maya quedó la fecha y nunca se supo del fulgor de esos maizales. Nadie sabe. Como el Perú se lloró; querido maizal, queridos cráteres. Reposa.

Nicho: país Colorado del desierto. Igual que nicho antes descrito. Igual que todos los pedregales. Por lápida en letras decía: Mi Dios es de caras oscuras. Largas llanuras cafés ondulaban, pero no era el viento, sino los tanques y la sed de amor que las movía. Pidieron, pero sólo el granate respondió y juntos cayeron en los cañones. Cayó el desierto del norte. Nicho 16. Querida arena roja, decía ahora.

Tumba Nicho Venezuela. Bolívar del nicho dice. Lápidas, fosas del tercer mundo, como una vez se los llamó a los países. Nichos del país americano, nuevo americano o países que al verdor sonrieron. Adiós dicen. Todos conforman el galpón nombrado. Negro fue, como las barras de las petroleras en el mar. Es el nicho Venezuela. Allí sólo descansa un humano. Petróleo no hay ni tierra. Maldita noche.

Nicho del Perú y serranías. Como todos referidos en Cuartel y Nave sobre los países dichos yace de Sendero Luminoso y miseria extrema. En aviones rugieron desde el Urubamba un camino de luz y los destrozados izaron sus velas cayendo. De cholai salió el quejido: –Ay malo de mi Perú, dice, todos son tumbas. Más que en otros lloraron y ahora es sueño y yace. Fue el 7 de los vistos, se gime.

Nicho Colombia y países blancos. Anotados en conjunto. Pasadizo, cuartel y número dicho. En sierras cayeron tableteando y todo el pueblo fue la muerte primera. Luego, cuando la ciudad M19 enrojeció el cielo, las montañas acompañaron a los caídos y así, de caídos y muertos, sólo una nevada fue la Colombia. Resta en paz, sonó el canto de amor a la blanca. Blanco es negro. Así sea, dice, y se llora.

Nicho del país Central. Poco a poco la luz iba sombreando y al llegar aquí cambió de color. Fue al caer la tarde. Los países se hundieron en silencio pero bajo sus nichos se oyeron los ríos y bajo los ríos el grito de los indios que huían. Luego vino el sangramiento y los ríos sonaron igual que los bombarderos rugiendo. Fin. Murió Santo Domingo, ríos, lagos y verdes selvas. Se lee: fuimos buenos.

Nicho Paraguay. Referido en Cuartel 13. También masacre entre países, guerras del Chaco, de la Plata, condominio y padecimientos. Yace ahora alambrado en nicho, pasadizo y tumba. Dice: descanso para el guaraní Marcos, y sonó todo el canto dice, el nicho. Dice: Canto de paz al Paraguay, canto al helicóptero abatido, al país Ipacaraí que mata con la caña. Todo esto acabado. El nicho dice día y sangró.

Nicho: queridos cielos el Caribe. Murieron y está consignado en pasadizo y cuarteles 12 y 13. Fue el último brillo sobre el horizonte, el último fulgor. Miles y miles de pedazos se arrastraban pidiendo, luego cantaron, finalmente subieron y vieron las tumbas abrirse. Como la inmensa luna el cielo brillo otro instante y se apagó. Fue el vacío, el paño negro del amor caribeño. En epitafio se dice: cubrió todo.

Nicho: bosques del país El Álamo. Ardió, cayeron y quedó referido sin nicho especial. En países quedaron y restos. Inmensos aviones arrasaron tocando el amor calcinado. De láseres, guerra química y pesadilla fueron los bosques ardiendo. Es lloro, se dice, fueron quemaduras. De cenizas es la carne, quedó escrito. De carne son las selvas, quedó escrito. De selvas son los cuerpos y calcinados, quedó escrito.

Países centrales que lloran. Murieron en fecha, época y nombre. Fueron todos habidos en Cuartel 12, en urnas que se indican y causas. Cuando crecieron en países humanos y animales interrumpieron los ríos pero fueron amigos. Interrumpieron la selva, pero fueron amigos. Interrumpieron la pesadilla y fueron como los días. Sucedió antes. Lloraron la noche y ahora yacen. Negra es la bomba. Amen.

Países sudamericanos que lloran. Habidos todos por día, padecimiento y países devoradores en nicho del Cuartel 13. De arenales, ciudades indias y mundos, levantaron las masacres y no hubo perdón, amistad ni ley. Murieron de hambre de amor en sueños que señalan y nombrados. Yacen y descansan en paz. Por noche fosforecen y largan lamento. Esta indicada procedencia y queja. Amen.

Nicho Arauco. Habido en Cuartel 13. Fueron largos valles negros como los desaparecidos otros. Se anotó así: aviones sureños surcaron el cielo y al bombardear sus propias ciudades brillaron un segundo y cayeron. Están dicho en cuarteles con tumba escrita y advertencia. En cal borraron los restos y sólo quedó la herida final. Amen. Todos rompieron en lágrimas. Amen. Fue dura la vista. Amen.

Nicho Amazona: de la oscuridad y juego de sombras remitido al Cuartel indicado con pasadizo y lugar. Fue pendencia y cruce con países peruanos y brasileños. Del encuentro quedó la sangre, los grandes desiertos Sao Paulo y el cielo Amazona, quedó dicho. Quedó dicho que fue un río de muerte y Paraguay. La sangre aún empuja su lápida. Dice: resta y queda. Amen. No dice fecha. No, sólo Cruz dice.

Nicho USA. Habido en Cuartel 12. Países del norte y remitidos a comerse entre ellos debido a sueños de escudos espaciales, asesinatos de negros y dominio. Abajo fueron el cielo y llamaron Hiroshima al país que ardía; países del Central, valles y tragadores chilenos. Son noches las tumbas y es toda la noche la tumba americana. Yace como el bisonte en paz. Fue frase Navajo. Quedó escrito, Amen.

Nicho Argentina. Galpón 13, nave remitida bajo el país Perú y sobre el país Chile. De tortura y tortura, desaparecimiento y exterminio quedó hueca como los países nombrados y la noche no tuvo donde caer ni el día. País desaparecido del horror tras los cuarteles. Desde allí el viento sopló sobre la pampa inexistente y apagándose se vieron las masacradas caras, Amen. Lápida 6. Piel blanca sólo dice.

En párrafos se lee y dice:

Los focos llenaban el camino. El amor de
padre y madre se lloraron todos y al abrirse las
puertas subiendo recomenzó la balada. De su
amor desaparecido recorrió hueco tras hueco,
fosa tras fosa, buscando los ojos que no en–
cuentra. De lápida en lápida, de lloro en lloro,
por nicherías fue, por sombras fue y fue así:

– Todos los muchachos míos están destrozados, es mi karma ¿no?

– Me empapo mucho y te quiero todo.

– Cantando, oh sí, cantando a su amor desaparecido.

– Cantando, oh sí sí, cantando a su amor desaparecido.

Argentina, Uruguay y los países chilenos del amor mío y desaparecido. Por escaleras se sube de un país a otro. Por ascensores se sube o por aviones del amor que también baja a las sombras y a veces sube. Allí andamos tú y yo. Allí andamos entre las fosas tú y yo hablándonos: ¿Me comiste? ¿por qué tenías hambre chileno me comiste?

¿No te apenaste? Flores del Central país cambiaron y era que yo me moría. De tu lado me morí y me pusieron arriba como los países argentinos están ubicados sobre los chilenos. Todos van subiendo unos sobre otros: Nichos del galpón americano y muerto se llaman. Nos murieron — digo – se la pena y se llaman.

Te quería, te quería tanto, dice, que toda la noche negra silbó y yo te sostuve con mi mano y lo viste. Es cosa sólo de muertos. Sí es cosa sólo de muertos el ver cada una de estas letras abriéndose en nichos. Letras, letritas, dice, tumbas del amor ido dice. Yo te sostuve con mi mano y lo viste. ¿Leíste las letras, las letritas?: Países idos dice.

Del amor desaparecido también se llaman los países. Enmurallados yacen como nosotros. Masacraron a los muchachos y los países se quedaron. Nosotros somos ellos, tiré. Fue duro. Algunos se apodan países del hambre, de los descampados centrales o bien USA en el país americano. Más atrás están los otros. Amor mio: somos nos comidos.

Fin. Y entonces:

.... Reventada entonces oh sí lindo pende oh sí linda pende te vi mas abajo y estamos los dos muertos es mi karma ¿no? Vamos lindo pende ven ahora a mirar lo que de amor te canta éste todo en lágrimas y flores sí ven conmigo ahora. Corte. Ven conmigo ahora mar mío de las estrellas. Corte. Oh sí lindo pendejo ven conmigo ahora. Corte. Ven ahora, lee y sigue. Corte. Y entonces:

– Blancos glaciares, sí hermano, sobre los techos se acercan.

– Murió mi chica, murió mi chico, desaparecieron todos.

Desiertos de amor.

Lloré así y canté. Aullando los perros perseguían a los muchachos y los guardias sitiaban. Lloré y más fuerte mientras los cuerpos caían. Blanco y negro lloré el canto, el canto a su amor desaparecido. Todo el desespero mío yo lloré. El pasto sube hasta las nicherías. Los muchachos paisa le dije ten; ten mi pena y se apaga.

Los países están muertos. Un Galpón se llama Sudamérica y el otro Norte. Tormento me dio la vista, dije abriéndome. El responso cantamos. Entera mi mala estrella canté entonces el canto a mi amor que se iba. Muchas cruces se llamaban e iban. Todos paisanos dije llorando se ha ido. Se fue, y yo no peno ni no peno.

Nostalgia cantamos por los países y por el país chileno. Procesión fue y sentencia, cruzamos los otros nichos y frente al del país nuestro estalló el salmo. Toda la pena. Entero el salmo cayó entonces sobre su amor que no estaba. De nostalgia toda la procesión se fue cantando así, por ellos, por los países muertos puse no, no dolía.

La Internacional de los países muertos creció subiendo y mi amor puse. Todo el amor paisa, todo el lloro mío sumé y sonó entonces la General de los países muertos. Así sangré yo la herida y al partir rojo sonó el canto al amor desaparecido. Todas estaban como abriéndose igual que fosas estas letritas, el grito el país puse no, no dolía.

– Cantando cantando a su amor desaparecido.

– Cantando cantando a su amor desaparecido.

– Sí hermosa pende mía, lindo pende mío, es mi karma ¿no?

– Todos los países mío y natales se llaman del amor mío, es mi lindo y caído.

– Todos están allí, en los nichos flotan

– Donde yacen los viejos galpones, las paredes muy altas con torres de

– T.V.

– Tú podrías aparecer en las pantallas, oh sí amor.

– En mis sueños enciendo el dial y allí apareces en blanco y negro.

– Digo: –ése es el chico que soñaba, ése es el chico que soñaba.

– Cuando despierto sólo hay heridos en un largo patio y cueros cabelludos

– colgando de las antenas.

– Oigan amigos —les grité– esas épocas ya pasaron. Sólo se rieron de mí.

– Marcaron a los muchachos y a bayonetazos les cortaron el pelo.

– ¿Fumas marihuana? ¿Aspiras neoprén? ¿Qué mierda fumas rojo

– asqueroso?

– Pero son lindos. Aún así yo me reglo de verlos, mojo la cama y fumo.

– Yo me enamoro de ellos, me regio y me pinto entera. Envuelta en lágrimas

– los saludo.

– pero todos sueñan hoy el sueño de la muerte, oh sí lindo chico.

– Grandes glaciares vienen a llevarse ahora los restos de nuestro amor.

– Grandes glaciares vienen a tragarse los nichos de nuestro amor.

– Las nicherías están unas frente a las otras.

– De lejos parecen bloques.

– Todo lo vi mientras me daban, pero me viré y mi guardián no pudo

– retenerme.

– Allí conocí los colores y vi al verdadero Dios gritando dentro de los

– helados galpones de concreto,

– aullando dentro de los fantasmales galpones de concreto,

– mojándome entera dentro de los imposibles galpones de concreto.

– Mula chilena —me insultaba mi madre– ya llegará también tu hora.

– Me viré por muchos lugares y vi a mis viejos sin salir de allí.

– Son como Dios.

– Pero ellos no saben que su cachorra se está muriendo de amor y golpes en

– los viejos galpones.

– Ahora me buscan pobres viejos ateridos.

– Preñándonos de gruesos escupitajos juntos, jóvenes y viejos,

– reventaremos.

–   Ay amor reventaremos.

–   Ay amor reventaremos.

– La generación sudaca canta folk, baila rock, pero todos se están muriendo

– con la vista vendada en la barriga de los galpones.

– En cada nicho hay un país, están allí, son los países sudamericanos.

– Grandes glaciares vienen a recogerlos.

– Pegado, pegado a las rocas, al mar y las montañas.

– Murió mi chica, murió mi chico, desaparecieron todos.

Desiertos de amor.

Nos descargaron cal y piedras encima.

Por un segundo temí que te hicieran daño.

Ay amor, cuando sentí el primer estrépito me pegué todavía un poco más a ti.

Fue algo. Sí seguro fue algo. Sentí las piedras aplastándote y yo creí que gritarías, pero no. El amor son las cosas que pasan. Nuestro amor muerto no pasa.

Me derrumbé a tu lado creyendo que era yo la que me arrojaba. El pasto estará creciendo me imagino. En verdad me gustan más las piedras creí, no, el pasto.

Creí que eras tú y era yo. Que yo aún vivía, pero al irme sobre ti algo de tu vida me desmintió.

Fue un segundo, porque después te doblaste tú también y el amor nos creció como los asesinatos.

Es dulce y no. Fue el último crujido y ya no hubo necesidad de moverse. Todo ahora se mueve.

Tus pupilas están fijas, pero cuatro ojos infinitamente abiertos ven más que dos.

Por eso nos vimos. Por eso hablamos, mientras con tu espinazo sostienes el mío. Y aunque que nadie lo verá, yo pensé que sería bueno esto, que está bien. Que sería.

Ahora todos son caídos menos nosotros los caídos.

Ahora todo el universo somos tú y yo menos tú y yo.

Tras los golpes, ya idos, nos desplazamos un poco y destrozada yo fui lo único que sentiste acercarse.

Nadie sabrá, porque eres tú al que busco, al que cuido. Llorona de ti tal vez seamos todos una sola cosa.

Yo ahora lo sé pero no importa

– Ay, grandes glaciares se acercan, grandes glaciares sobre los techos de nuestro amor.

– Eh ronca, gritó mi lindo, los dinosaurios se levantan. Los helicópteros

– bajan y bajan

– Recorrí muchas partes.

– Mis amigos sollozaban dentro de los viejos galpones de concreto.

– Los muchachos aullaban.

– Vamos, hermos llegado donde nos decían —le grité a mi lindo chico.

– Goteando de la cara me acompañaban los Sres.

– Pero a nadie encontré para decirle "buenos días", sólo unos brujos con

– máuser ordenándome una bien sangrienta.

– Yo les dije — están locos, ellos dijeron — no lo creas.

– Sólo las cruces se veían y los viejos galpones cubiertos de algo.

– De un bayonetazo me cercenaron el hombro y sentí mi brazo al caer al

– pasto.

– Y luego con él golpearon a mis amigos.

– Siguieron y siguieron, pero cuando les empezaron a dar a mis padres corrí al

– urinario a vomitar.

– Inmensas praderas se formaban en cada una de las arcadas, las nubes

– rompiendo el cielo y los cerros acercándose.

– Cómo te llamas y qué haces me preguntaron.

– Mira tiene un buen cul. Cómo te llamas buen culo bastarda chica, me

– preguntaron.

– Pero mi amor ha quedado pegado a las rocas, al mar y a las montañas.

– Pero mi amor te digo, ha quedado adherido a las rocas, a mar y a las

– montañas.

– Ellas no conocen los malditos galpones de concreto.

– Ellas son. Yo vengo con mis amigos sollozando.

– Yo vengo de muchos lugares.

– Yo vengo llorando. Fumo y pongo con los chicos.

– Es bueno para ver colores.

– Pero nos están cavando frente a las puertas.

– Pero todo será nuevo, te digo,

– oh sí lindo pende.

– Claro —dijo el guardia, hay que arrancar el cáncer de raíz,

– oh sí, oh sí.

– El hombro cortado me sangraba y era el olor raro la sangre.

– Dando vuelta se ven los dos enormes galpones.

– Marcas de T.N.T., guardias y gruesas alambradas cubren sus vidrios rotos.

– Pero a nosotros nunca nos hallarán porque nuestro amor está pegado a

– las rocas al mar y a las montañas.

– Pegado, pegado a las rocas, al mar y las montañas.

–Vi gente desgreñada, hombres picoteados de viruela y miles de cruces en la

–nevera, oh sí, oh sí.

–Moviendo las piernas a todos esos podridos tíos invoqué.

–Todo se había borrado menos los dos malditos galpones.

–Rey un perverso de la cintura quiso tomarme, pero aymara el número de

–mi guardián puse sobre el pasto y huyó.

–Despés me vendaron la vista. Vi a la virgen, vi a Jesús, vi a mi madre

–despellejándome a golpes.

–En la oscuridad te busqué, pero nada pueden ver los chicos lindos bajo la

–venda de los ojos.

–Yo vi a la virgen vi a Satán y al señor K.

–Todo estaba secos frente a los nichos de concreto.

–El teniente dijo "vamos", pero yo busco y lloré por mi muchacho.

–   Ay amor.

–Maldición, dijo el teniente, vamos a colorear un poco.

–Murió mi chica, murió mi chico, desaparecieron todos.

                                        Desiertos de amor.

Ay amor, quebrados caímos y en la caída lloré mirándote. Fue golpe tras golpe, pero los últimos ya no eran necesarios. Apenas un poco nos arrastramos entre los cuerpos caídos para quedar juntos, para quedar uno al lado del otro. No es duro ni la soledad, nada ha sucedido y mi sueño se levanta y cae como siempre. Como los días. Como la noche. Todo mi amor está aquí y se ha quedado:

– *Pegado a las rocas, al mar y a las montañas.*

– *Pegado, pegado, a las rocas al mar y a las montañas*

Canté, canté de amor, con la cara toda bañada canté de amor y los muchachos me sonrieron. Más fuerte canté, la pasión puse, el sueño, la lágrima. Canté la canción de los viejos galpones de concreto. Unos sobre otros decenas de nichos los llenaban. En cada uno hay un país, son como niños, están muertos. Todos yacen allí, países negros, África y sudacas. Yo les canté así de amor la pena a los países.Miles de cruces llenaban hasta el fin el campo. Entera su enamorada canté así. Canté el amor:

Fue el tormento, los golpes, y en pedazos nos rompimos. Yo alcancé a oírte pero la luz se iba. Te busqué entre los destrozados, hablé contigo. Tus restos me miraron y yo te abrace. Todo acabó. No queda nada. Pero muerta te amo y nos amamos aunque esto nadie pueda entenderlo.

— Sí, sí, miles de cruces llenaban hasta el fin el campo.
— Llegué desde los sitios más lejanos, con toneladas de cerveza adentro y
— ganas de desaguar.
— Así llegué a los viejos galpones de concreto.
— De cerca eran cuarteles abovedados, con sus vidrios rotos y olor a pichí,
— semen, sangre y moco hedían.

A la paisa

A las madres de la plaza de mayo

A la agrupación de los familiares de los que no aparecen

A todos los tortura, palomos del amor, países chilenos y asesinos

Ahora Zurita — me largó — ya que de puro ver-
so y desgarro te pudiste entrar aquí, en nuestras
pesadillas: ¿tú puedes decirme donde está mi hijo?

CANTO A SU
AMOR
DESAPARECIDO

CANTO A SU AMOR DESAPARECIDO

SONG FOR HIS DISAPPEARED LOVE

BY RAÚL ZURITA

TRANSLATED BY DANIEL BORZUTZKY

ACTION BOOKS

NOTRE DAME, INDIANA 2010